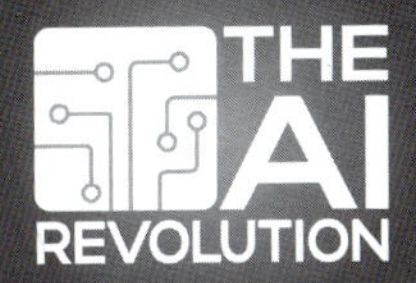

THE TROUBLE WITH DEEPFAKES

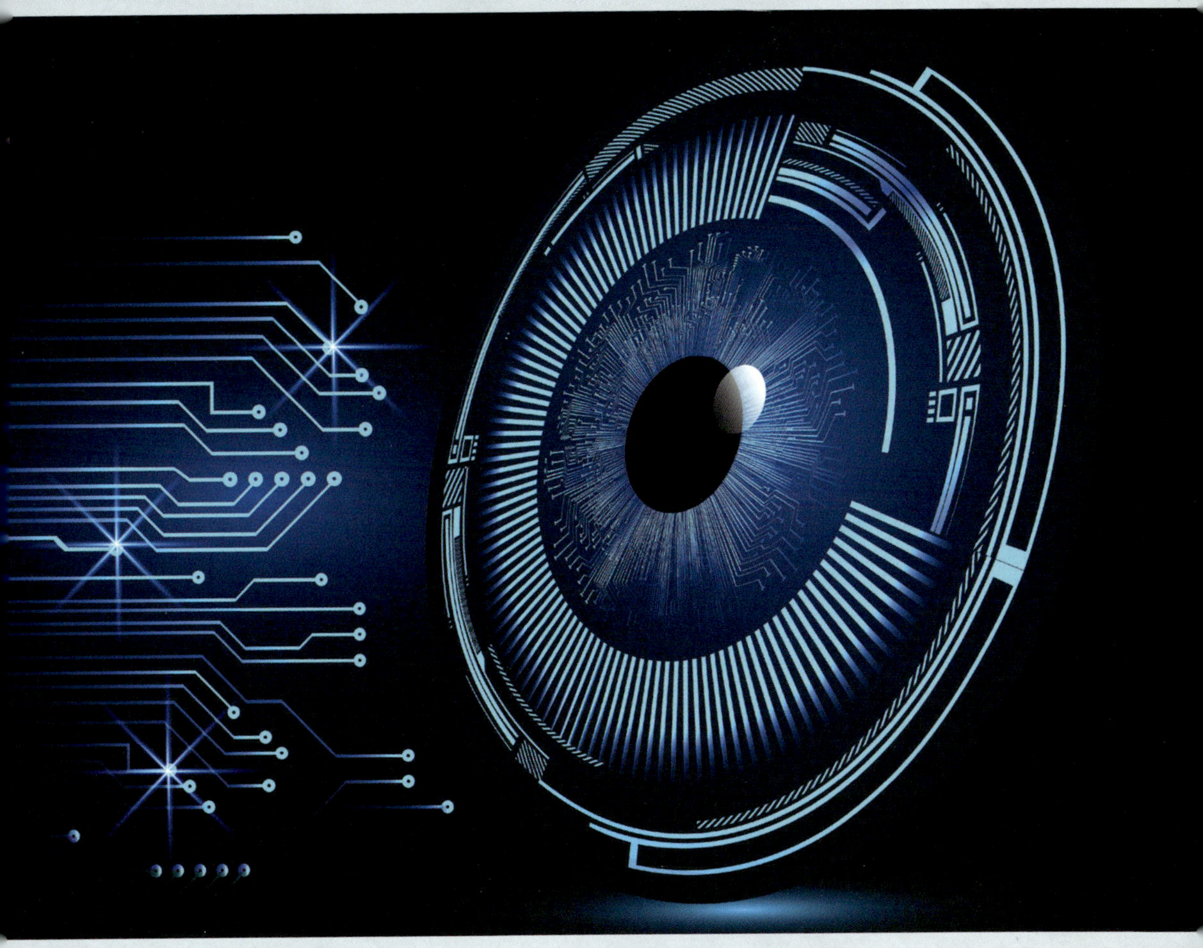

by Josh Gregory

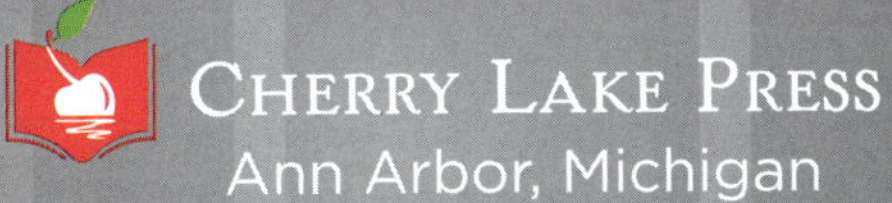

Published in the United States of America by Cherry Lake Publishing
Ann Arbor, Michigan
www.cherrylakepublishing.com

Reading Adviser: Beth Walker Gambro, MS, Ed., Reading Consultant, Yorkville, IL

Photo Credits: © titima037/Freepik.com, cover, title page; © Consolidated News Photos/Shutterstock, 5; © FAMILY STOCK/Shutterstock, 6; © FlixPix / Alamy Stock Photo, 9; © Pop Nukoonrat/Dreamstime.com, 11; © Dedmityay/Dreamstime.com, 13; © Luca Lorenzelli/Dreamstime.com, 14; Georgejmclittle/Dreamstime.com, 17; © gowithstock/Dreamstime.com, 19; © Lightfieldstudiosprod/Dreamstime.com, 21; © Noiel/Shutterstock, 25; © Iurii Motov/Shutterstock, 26; © Tongsupatman/Dreamstime.com, 27; © Linaimages/Shutterstock, 29

Cherry Lake Press is an imprint of Cherry Lake Publishing Group.

Library of Congress Cataloging-in-Publication Data has been filed and is available at catalog.loc.gov.

Cherry Lake Press would like to acknowledge the work of the Partnership for 21st Century Learning, a Network of Battelle for Kids. Please visit Battelle for Kids online for more information.

Printed in the United States of America

ABOUT THE AUTHOR

Josh Gregory is the author of more than 200 books for kids. He has written about everything from animals to technology to history. A graduate of the University of Missouri–Columbia, he currently lives in Chicago, Illinois.

CONTENTS

Chapter 1

FACT OR FICTION

Imagine you're surfing YouTube. You're looking at the recommended videos. You see there's an important news announcement from the president. It looks very official. The president is standing behind a **podium**. He's looking serious. He's talking about a war. But something weird happens after a few moments. The president suddenly starts dancing. He's rapping the lyrics to a popular song. What's going on here?

It turns out you weren't watching a video of the president at all. Instead, it was something called a deepfake. Deepfakes are realistic-looking videos. They seem to show people saying and doing things they never said or did. These videos are created using powerful artificial intelligence (AI) technology. Many people create them. They usually post them online as jokes. But others create deepfakes that are truly meant to fool people. These creators want to cause trouble.

This is a real photo of President Joe Biden. But it's easier than ever for people to make realistic fake pictures and videos of public figures.

The idea of trying to fool people using fake images is not new. Before computers, people would sometimes alter photos by hand. These might be printed in untrustworthy newspapers or magazines. Most people knew not to trust them. But others simply believed their eyes. Computers eventually made it even easier to alter a digital image. Just a few clicks could put a celebrity's face on the body of someone making a rude gesture.

There are already widely-used apps that allow people to digitally switch faces. Altering digital images is easier than ever before.

In the 2010s, technology pushed this kind of **misinformation** to a new level. Convincing fake videos of celebrities started to pop up online. Starting in 2017, people began calling them "deepfakes." These videos have become more widespread since then. It is easy to find them all over social media. Often, they are mixed with real videos.

You may not have seen these videos yourself. But you have probably heard about them. They are a big topic in the news. Deepfakes might seem like harmless fun at first. Could it really hurt anyone to make a TikTok video of a famous actor saying something silly? Unfortunately, not all deepfakes are created to entertain. Some of them can cause big problems. People are worried.

DEEPFAKE MOVIE MAGIC

The technology behind deepfakes isn't just used to fool people or make jokes online. You might even see it on the big screen. It is used in the latest big-budget movies. Filmmakers have used it to do things like make older actors look like younger versions of themselves. In a recent *Star Wars* movie, you can see actors who died years ago. They are delivering new lines alongside living actors. This was done using repurposed, unused footage from previous movies. Deepfake technology could be used for this same purpose. It could create brand new footage of actors who died years ago. One day, it might even be possible to create entire movies without any human actors at all.

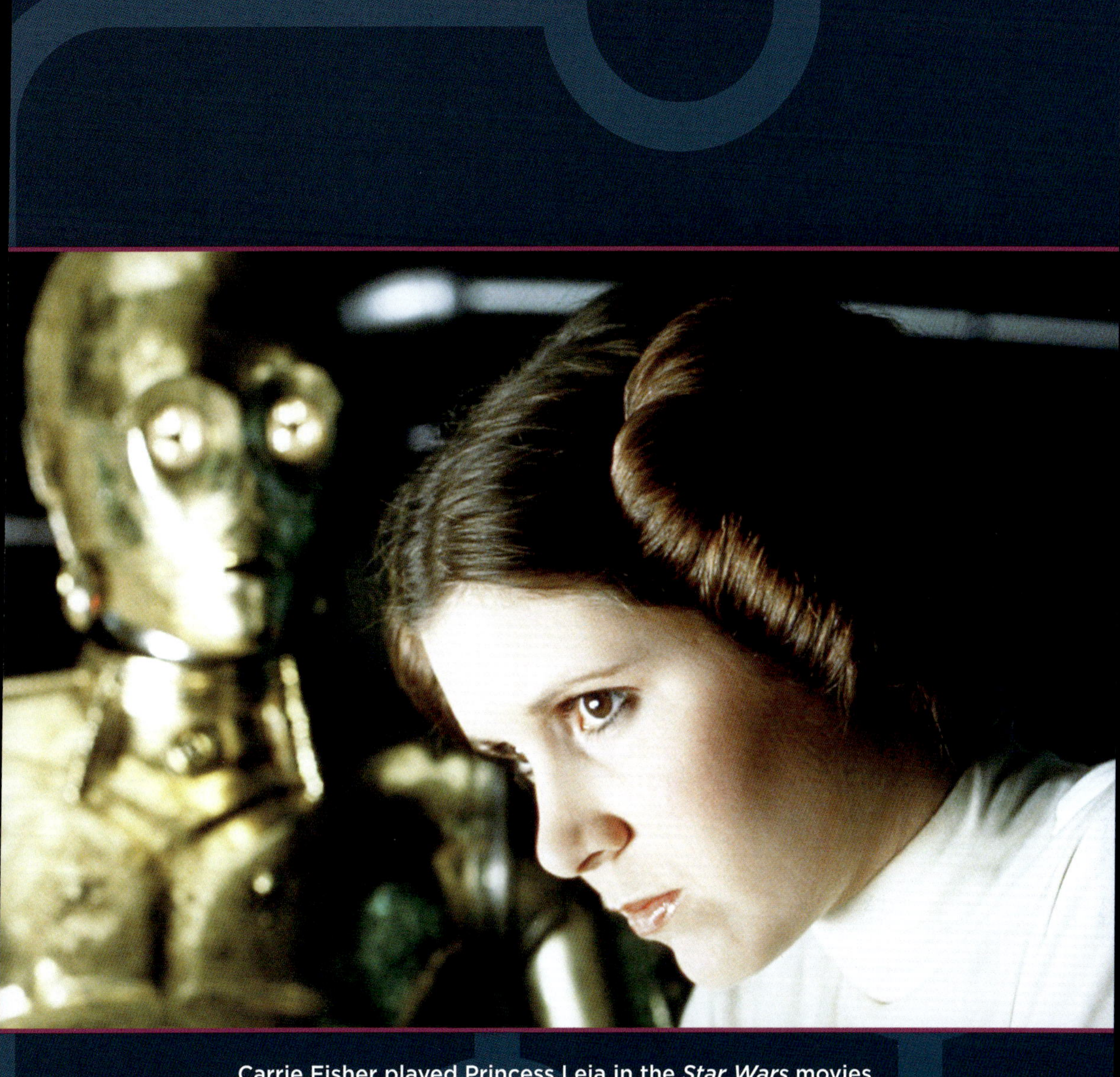

Carrie Fisher played Princess Leia in the *Star Wars* movies. Carrie Fisher passed away in 2016. Footage of her was used in the 2019 movie *Star Wars: The Rise of Skywalker*.

Chapter 2

HOW IT WORKS

Deepfakes got their name from the type of AI technology that powers them. It's called "deep learning." A deep learning system requires an **algorithm** and a lot of **data**. An algorithm is a set of steps. A computer can follow these steps to solve a problem or complete a task. In deep learning, the algorithm's task is to seek out patterns in data. Data can be anything from videos and photos to text or audio recordings. The system's creators feed huge amounts of data into the algorithm. The system then starts to "learn" things about that data.

Think of the way you learn things. For example, studying flash cards might help you learn new words. You remember better as you study more. Deep learning is a lot like that. An AI's creators give it more and more data. Then the system gets better at noticing and remembering things about that data.

"Deep learning" is a type of machine learning.

How does this lead to deepfakes? Imagine a system that has viewed hundreds of hours of videos of a certain person talking. It slowly starts to pick up the details of that person's movements. How their mouth moves. How their eyebrows raise when they get excited. Where the creases and folds are on their face. And many even tinier details that make each person unique.

Now imagine another system that is doing the same thing. This one uses audio recordings of the person's voice. It starts to notice exactly what they sound like as they say certain words. It figures out how their voice changes as they get excited.

Eventually, these systems are experts. They are able to create their own video and audio. People can simply type what they want the deepfake to say. Or they might record an actor doing an impression of the person. Then they can use the deepfake system to make the impression sound more realistic. This audio is then combined with a deepfake video. The person's mouth and face move to look like they are saying the words in the deepfake audio. The results can be very realistic.

AI voice assistants are already widely used. AI learning and being able to copy the voices they hear is the next step.

Not just anyone can make a deepfake. Good ones require powerful computers and special programs. They also require a lot of data. That's why most deepfakes are of people like presidents or movie stars. A lot of video and audio footage of those people is available. Deepfake systems are getting better all the time, though. They require less and less data to learn. They can produce more realistic videos faster than ever before. The best deepfake programs are not even available to the public. They are carefully controlled by deep learning researchers. But deepfakes are still becoming more common. And they are better than ever.

Face swap apps are very common. AI recognizes faces and swaps them in the frame.

ON THE BRIGHT SIDE

Sometimes deepfake technology can be put to positive use. Some illnesses cause people to lose their ability to talk. These people rely on computerized voices to speak for them. But deepfake voice technology can help them keep their old voices. They make recordings of their voice while they are still able to talk. These recordings are fed into a deep learning system. It creates a record of what the voice sounded like. The deepfake version of the person's voice can then be used in place of the computer voice. It's a lot like the way you can change the way Siri's voice sounds on an iPhone. In this case, it's a real person's voice!

Chapter 3

RUINED REPUTATIONS

Trustworthy news and information are extremely important. People need these things to learn about the world. Good information helps them make important decisions. It helps people decide who to vote for and which causes to support. It also helps them choose which products to buy and which to avoid. It might help them decide what kinds of jobs they want. It could even help them decide where to live.

Misinformation is common online. Fake news stories spread easily on social media. Many people read and believe these stories. And now much of this fake news comes from deepfake videos. Some people think that this will lead to people distrusting all videos, including real ones.

Deepfake images, audio, and videos can make it more difficult for people to tell which stories online are real and which are fake.

Many people use misinformation to try and influence politics. Deepfakes can be used to spread lies about people running for office. For example, there could be a deepfake video of a politician saying something offensive. It could keep people from voting for the candidate.

Some of the first people affected by deepfakes were movie stars and other celebrities. These kinds of videos can be fun for fans. But sometimes they can also be hurtful. A deepfake could show a celebrity doing something embarrassing. It could hurt their career. Or it might lead to a star's young fans seeing something inappropriate when they click on a video.

Deepfakes don't affect only famous people. For example, a deepfake of a real person's voice could be used to make phone calls to their relatives. The caller could then scam those people out of money. It could get them to give up private information. Or imagine if someone created a deepfake using someone's YouTube vlogs or TikTok videos. This could lead to someone making embarrassing deepfakes of everyday people.

Many people post videos of themselves online. Deepfakes could be made using these videos of regular people.

Some deepfakes don't feature real people at all. That doesn't mean they don't cause problems of their own. Some clips posted online have real-looking news anchors. They are delivering real-looking news. But nothing about them is real. The people are entirely computer-generated. They are created using deepfake AI technology. But they are not meant to look like well-known people. They are just meant to look like they are hosting a real news broadcast. Sometimes this is all it takes to fool people and spread lies.

Deepfakes don't only spread misinformation. They also create another problem. If people know that some videos are deepfakes, they might not trust any videos. They might feel like there's no such thing as trustworthy information. It then becomes harder for people to understand what's happening in the world and make decisions.

ASK AN AI

Let's go straight to the source and ask the AI text generator ChatGPT what it thinks of deepfakes.

Hi, ChatGPT
Hello! How can I assist you today?

Why are deepfakes such a problem today?
Deepfakes are a big problem because they use advanced technology to make fake videos or audio that look and sound real. This can spread false information, harm people's reputations, and mess with what we trust online. As this technology gets better, it's harder to tell what's real and what's fake. Solving this issue needs better tech, more awareness, and rules to stop the harm caused by fake content.

What can we do to solve this?

To deal with deepfakes, first get better tech to spot fake stuff. Teach people to be careful online and know about deepfakes. Make sure AI is used the right way with clear rules. Put in and follow rules to stop bad use of deepfake tech. Get tech experts, researchers, and leaders working together. Make online identity checks stronger to avoid fakes. Lastly, tell people to be honest when making and sharing stuff online. By doing these things, we can handle deepfakes better and protect folks from their impact.

Thanks for sharing your thoughts!

You're welcome! If you have any more questions or if there's anything else I can help you with, feel free to ask.

(This conversation has been slightly edited and condensed for space.)

Chapter 4

DEFENDING AGAINST DEEPFAKES

Deepfakes aren't going to suddenly disappear from the internet. The technology already exists. People will find ways to use it. But there are things we can all do to stop deepfakes from having a negative impact on our world.

One way to fight deepfakes is to learn some ways to spot them. Some signs are fairly easy to see. Maybe the person's lips aren't quite matching the words you hear. You might notice strange shadows on a person's face. They don't look quite right. Or a person's skin might look too smooth. They might look almost like a video game character. These can all be hints that a video is a deepfake. Be careful, though. Even real videos sometimes look a little odd. It doesn't necessarily mean the video is fake. And some fakes are very good. You might have a hard time noticing any flaws.

Sometimes it's very difficult to tell if something online is a deepfake. Some lawmakers are fighting to make laws surrounding deepfakes online.

Check who posted the video. Does it come from a known, trustworthy news source? Or was it posted by a random stranger on social media? Not sure about something you see online? Always check the source. Look for videos posted by respected news sources and other trustworthy organizations. They will avoid posting deepfakes and other misinformation.

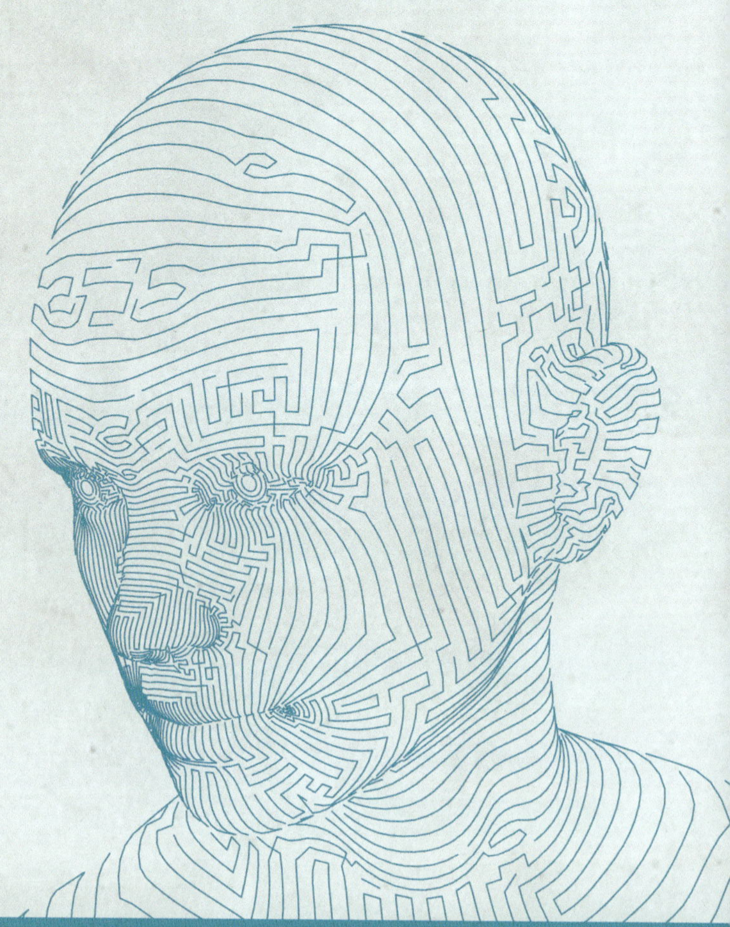

New consent laws for deepfakes may include people having to check consent boxes when uploading videos of themselves.

New laws should also help combat the growing deepfake problem. Some lawmakers have already proposed laws that would make it illegal to post a deepfake of someone without their **consent**. Others have suggested that all deepfake videos should have a special mark on them. This mark would tell people they are fake.

Deepfakes will continue to get better. They will continue changing the way people share information online. People will need to take care and educate themselves more than ever. Staying informed will be the best first step you can take.

AI vs. AI

One solution to the deepfake problem could be using specially trained AI programs to fight back. Researchers are working to create AI systems that can detect even the most convincing deepfakes. Researchers hope these systems will be able to work as filters on social media or video streaming sites. They could automatically recognize deepfakes and block them from being posted. This would help cut down on the misinformation being spread online.

ACTIVITY:

A CLOSER LOOK

Think of a celebrity you'd like to know more about. With an adult, look up five articles or videos about this person. Take a close look at these sources to see if they are trustworthy. Here are some things to check:

- Who wrote the article or made the video? Does it come from a well-known source? Is it straight from the celebrity themself? Or is it something made by a fan?
- Does the article or video have a lot of views? Who is commenting on it? What kinds of things are they writing?
- Do the five sources say the same things about the person? Or does one of them stick out as different?
- Do the articles and videos contain direct quotes from the celebrity? Or is it just someone else's opinions?
- Do the articles or videos explain where they got their information about the person?

FIND OUT MORE

Books

Abell, Tracy. *Artificial Intelligence Ethics and Debates.* Lake Elmo, MN: Focus Readers, 2020.

Felix, Rebecca. *Artificial Intelligence: Can Computers Take Over?* Minneapolis, MN: Checkerboard Library, 2019.

Hudak, Heather C. *Misinformation, Disinformation, and Censorship.* New York, NY: Crabtree Publishing, 2024.

Mattern, Joanne. *All about Artificial Intelligence.* Lake Elmo, MN: Focus Readers, 2023.

On the Web

Search these online sources with an adult:

"Artificial Intelligence." Britannica for Kids.

"Be MediaWise: How to detect deepfakes and avoid disinformation." PBS Newshour Classroom.

"ChatGPT." OpenAI.

"Fakeout." TIME for Kids.

"Public opinion facts for kids." Kiddle.

"What is artificial intelligence (AI)?" IBM.

GLOSSARY

algorithm (AL-guh-rih-thuhm)
a series of steps that can be followed to achieve a certain goal

consent (kuhn-SENT)
permission to do something

data (DAY-tuh)
information used to create, process, or support something

misinformation (miss-in-fuhr-MAY-shuhn)
false information that is spread on purpose, often online

podium (POH-dee-uhm)
a structure on a raised platform; people often stand behind them to give speeches

INDEX